GERMAN DESTROYERS AND ESCORTS

A *Narvik* Class destroyer (*Z24*)—one of Erdmenger's famous flotilla—lying at anchor and showing off the 15 cm twin C38 turret and the radar aerial over the bridge. The girdle-like attachment, which runs along the hull beneath the first row of scuttles and then along the bulwark, is a degaussing coil (262/1522/15a).

PAUL BEAVER

GERMAN DESTROYERS AND ESCORTS

WORLD WAR 2 PHOTO ALBUM NUMBER 20

A selection of German wartime photographs from the Bundesarchiv, Koblenz

PSL **Patrick Stephens, Cambridge**

First published in 1981

British Library Cataloguing in Publication Data

German destroyers and escorts. – (World War 2
  photo albums; no 20)
  1. World War, 1939–45 – Naval operations,
  German
  2. Destroyers (Warships) – Germany – History
  3. Destroyers escorts – Germany – History
  I. Beaver, Paul   II. Series
  940.54′5943   D771

  ISBN 0 85059 458 8 (casebound)
  ISBN 0 85059 459 6 (softbound)

Photoset in 10pt Plantin Roman. Printed in Great
Britain on 100 gsm Fineblade coated cartridge and
bound by The Garden City Press Limited,
Letchworth, Hertfordshire SG6 1JS, for the
publishers, Patrick Stephens Limited, Bar Hill,
Cambridge, CB3 8EL, England.

CONTENTS

Acknowledgements
The author and publisher would like to express their sincere thanks to Mrs Marianne Loenartz of the Bundesarchiv for her assistance, without which this book would have been impossible.

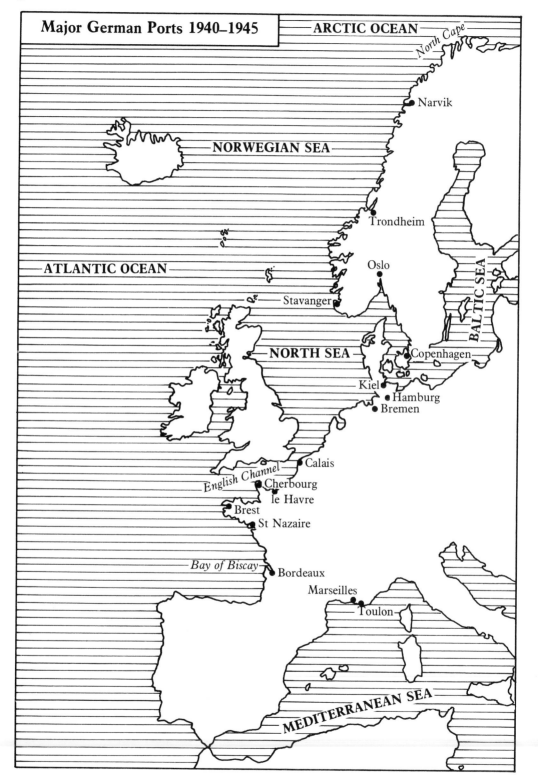

Major German Ports 1940–1945

ARCTIC OCEAN

North Cape

● Narvik

NORWEGIAN SEA

● Trondheim

ATLANTIC OCEAN

Oslo ●

Stavanger ●

NORTH SEA

BALTIC SEA

● Copenhagen

Kiel ●

● Hamburg

● Bremen

Calais ●

English Channel ● Cherbourg

le Havre ●

● Brest

● St Nazaire

Bay of Biscay ● Bordeaux

Marseilles ●

● Toulon

MEDITERRANEAN SEA

The destroyers and torpedo boats of the Kriegsmarine, although not fully utilised during World War 2, were fundamental workhorses and served in many roles in most theatres. Together with the ocean-going minesweepers, also covered in this volume, they provided cover for capital ships and coastal convoys and thus were an inextricable part of the German maritime operations, as covered in the previous three volumes relating to warships in this series.

The Treaty of Versailles had left the Kaiserliche Marine with only 16 destroyers – the so-called torpedo-boat destroyers of World War 1. In fact, the Germans had a habit of calling all small warships by the general name *Zerstörer*, and this can confuse the naval historian on occasions! Under the terms of the Treaty, only a dozen of these craft could be operated at one time, together with a similar number of torpedo boats (Torpedoboote).

In 1934, with the re-emergence of German nationalism, the destroyer force, by then hopelessly outdated, began a rebuilding programme. This programme was initially conducted in great secrecy because Adolf Hitler did not repudiate the Treaty of Versailles until March 1935. The first designs were for 2,270-ton destroyers with 5 × 1 128 mm (5-inch) main armament and eight torpedo tubes apiece. This was, of course, totally contrary to the Versailles agreement, but the Western Powers stood by and watched the threat build up. Further building was put in hand with five units being launched in 1935 and seven in 1936. These destroyers were of the 1934 type and were followed by the 1936 type, for as war clouds gathered over Europe more and more of these 'greyhounds' were ordered, their tonnages slowly creeping up. The famous Z-Plan called for 58 destroyers and 90 torpedo boats to be built by 1948, and by the commencement of hostilities in 1939, 20 of each type had been completed.

The Kriegsmarine (the name was changed on May 21 1935) realised that the Royal and French Navies were in an overwhelmingly dominant position in regard to quantity of destroyer types, but the Germans had the edge in respect of quality. Although basically simple in design, German destroyers of the 1936A type were the largest design to serve in World War 2 toting 150 mm (5.9-inch) guns and displacing over 3,600 tons fully loaded.

The 1936A (Mob) type (or class) were fitted with a supposedly lightweight forward twin gun turret, but this modern-looking mounting caused considerable problems in service conditions. The problems were, in fact, so severe that the Senior Officer of the 8th Destroyer Flotilla (Flotilla Narvik) felt it necessary to write to the Oberkommando der Marine in Berlin. In his report Kapitän zur See Erdmenger complained bitterly about the seakeeping problems which led to a high crew fatigue rate, especially in that infamous forward turret which still had to be hand loaded. He, like many other destroyer commanders, thought the single A&B mountings of other types to be superior.

Another problem encountered with Kriegsmarine destroyers was the unreliability of the high-pressure boilers originally fitted to the training ships *Bremse* and *Brummer* before the war. These boilers had a bad habit of breaking down just when a Captain needed full steam.

During the hostilities, the armament of all destroyers was amended, usually to give more anti-aircraft protection – some of the larger units were equipped with up to 16 20 mm and four 37 mm ack-ack guns. The bow shape was also altered on a number of ships to give better sea handling characteristics – a quality very necessary in the rough and dangerous Polar seas frequented by several destroyer flotillas. In these waters it was not only the Allies who were the enemy but the weather as well – even more so. Ice would often form on a destroyer's upper works making them top-heavy, difficult to handle and impossible to fight effectively.

The German destroyer forces started the war under the control of Flag Officer, Torpedo Boats (Führer der Torpedoboote), who was himself subject to the C-in-C Reconnaissance Forces (Befehlshaber der Aufklärungsstreitkrafte). Operational conditions brought about a change in the organisation, however, and the new post of Flag Officer, Destroyers (Führer der Zerstörer or FdZ) was created in November 1939. The new organisation, reporting to the Fleet Commander (Flottenchef), was divided into six flotillas with many famous commanders such as Erich Bey, who as a Konter-Admiral lost his life at North Cape in December 1943.

The first real action of the destroyer forces was not until October 1939, when nine units were sent to escort capital ships attempting to draw out the British Home Fleet. An operation which ended without success on either side. Later in the month, destroyers under Konter-Admiral Lütjens (Führer der Torpedoboote), the Flag Officer of the ill-fated *Bismarck* sortie in May 1941, carried out an offensive mining operation off the Humber which resulted in the loss of several Allied merchant ships. These cat and mouse actions continued for some time but they were not always successful for the Kriegsmarine. For example, in February 1940 Heinkel bombers of KG26 mistakenly attacked destroyers of the First Flotilla engaged in Operation Wikinger under the FdZ. Unfortunately for the Kriegsmarine, north-west of Borkum, *Z1 Leberecht Maass* was hit by three bombs and, whilst taking evasive action, *Z3 Max Schultz* collided with a mine, probably laid by its own forces. Both warships and most of their crews were lost.

Despite this setback, nearly all the operational destroyers were used extensively in the opening stages of Operation Weserübung, the invasion of Denmark and Norway. Within a matter of days, however, one class almost ceased to exist. So drastic was this loss that the destroyer command structure had to be altered yet again.

In the early morning of April 10 1940, the British 2nd Destroyer Flotilla under Captain Warburton-Lee entered Ofotfjord, damaging two large destroyers and sinking two more including *Z21 Wilhelm Heidkamf*, flagship of the FdZ and under the command of Korvetten-Kapitän Erdmenger. Three days later, another sortie was made into the Norwegian fjords by a squadron led by HMS *Warspite* – the Second Battle of Narvik had begun. The battleship's Swordfish floatplane flew up the long fjord and established the hiding place of the German destroyers and U-boats, mainly in Rombaksfjord. Casualties included *Z18 Hans Lüdemann*, (commanded by Korvetten-Kapitän Friedrichs) which had to be scuttled as a result of a torpedo attack by HMS *Eskimo*, and *Z22 Anton Schmitt* (commanded by Korvetten-Kapitän Böhme) which was torpedoed and

sunk by the British destroyers. At the end of the day, ten destroyers were on the bottom but these losses did not stop the Germans from occupying Norway and setting up naval bases along the coast. These bases were later used to harass British convoys to Russia.

With the fall of France, new bases were opened up to the Kriegsmarine with destroyers now able to operate from Cherbourg, Brest and Bordeaux. Operations in the Mediterranean theatre were carried out by captured or seconded destroyers, warships such as the *Hermes*, an ex-Hellenic destroyer, and Italian vessels taken over in 1943. Dutch and Norwegian destroyers and escorts were also taken over and had very often to be raised after their own crews had scuttled them.

Following the loss of the destroyers at Narvik, the famous 8th Narvik Flotilla was formed in December 1940 under the command of Kapitän zur See Pönitz until March 1943, when our old friend Hans Erdmenger took over. The flotilla consisted of the destroyers *Z23* to *Z30*, which were fitted with the new turret mentioned previously. The only unit not fitted with the mountings was *Z26* which was sunk, before the guns were available, by gunfire from HMSs *Trinidad* and *Eclipse* during a North Sea encounter in March 1942 (see below).

In early February 1942, the famous two-day Channel Dash, known to the Germans as Operation Cerberus, by three Kriegsmarine capital ships transferring from Brest to German ports, via the English Channel, took place. This notable cock-a-snook at the Royal Navy could not have been possible without a considerable effort on the part of the smaller warships of the Kriegsmarine. Many days of intense minesweeping was carried out by the 1st, 2nd, 4th, 5th, and 12th Minesweeper Flotillas (Minensuchflotille) with Raümboot escorts (see *E-boats and Coastal Craft* in this series). Close escort for the capital ships – *Scharnhorst, Gneisenau* and *Prinz Eugen* – was provided by FdZ (Konter-Admiral Bey) with the 5th Destroyer Flotilla (Kapitän zur See Berger) consisting of the warships *Z29* and *Z25* (1936A type), and the smaller 1934 type destroyers *Z4 Richard Beitzen, Z5 Paul Jacobi, Z7 Hermann Schoemann* and *Z14 Friedrich Ihn*. These forces were later joined by two torpedo boat flotillas – the 2nd from Le Havre (Fregatten-Kapitän Erdmann) and the 3rd from Dunkirk (Fregatten-Kapitän

Wilke). This latter flotilla was joined by four older, 1923 type torpedo boats from the 5th Flotilla off Dover on February 12. The British had been caught napping by this bold operation and the only serious casualty on the German side was the minesweeper *M1208* which was lost during the preparatory sweeps a few nights before the actual Dash. Both battle cruisers, although damaged by mines laid off the Dutch coast, reached their havens in Germany on February 13 (see *German Capital Ships* in this series).

Luck did not always run with the destroyers, though, as events six weeks later off the Norwegian coast showed. Seeking a convoy bound for Russia, the 8th Flotilla (Kapitän zur See Pönitz) headed out into the Norwegian Sea. They unluckily did not find *PQ13*, but rather its escort force led by the cruiser HMS *Trinidad*. In absolutely appalling weather *Z26*, a 3,500 tons, 1936A, launched in 1940 was sunk, but her sister ships in the same half-flotilla, *Z24* and *Z25* escaped. The weather again played havoc with another attempt to hit the next Murmansk bound convoy, *PQ14* and although the U-boat Arm and the Luftwaffe found the ships, the destroyer flotilla ordered to engage in surface action had to return to base, unable to locate the convoy, or even to keep station in the severe icing conditions. In late April and early May, a return convoy, *QP11*, was attacked in the Barents Sea by destroyers under the command of Kapitän zur See Schulze aboard the 6th Flotilla's leader, *Z7 Hermann Schoemann*. On May 1, *Z7* succeeded in engaging and damaging the flagship of the convoy's close escort, the cruiser HMS *Edinburgh*, resulting in the loss of both ships. Not before, however, the commander of *Z24*, Korvetten-Kapitän Saltzwedel, had shown just how courageous and skilful German destroyer crews were by successfully coming alongside the stricken destroyer and taking off the crew whilst *Z25* (Korvetten-Kapitän Peters) used smoke to cover the operation.

Another tough engagement was fought on the last day of 1942, when Operation Regenbogen, another anti-convoy skirmish, led to the demise of *Z16 Friedrich Echoldt*, the last 1934 type to be built. Whilst escorting the heavy cruiser *Admiral Hipper*, *Z4 Richard Beitzen*, *Z16* and *Z29* sank HMS *Bramble*, before the heavier British warships arrived on the scene. During the withdrawal from action, Korvetten-Kapitän Bachmann in *Z16* closed with a capital ship he took to be the *Hipper*. Unfortunately, its silhouette changed into the shape of HMS *Sheffield*, the close escort's flagship. *Z16* was promptly sunk with all hands and there was nothing *Admiral Hipper*'s force could do but withdraw to Altenfjord, leaving the merchant ships of the convoy untouched.

Late 1943 saw an increase in destroyer operations in the Bay of Biscay area as German merchant blockade runners tried to bring home valuable cargoes of raw materials unobtainable in Europe.

The first of these operations was staged on Christmas Eve 1943 and called Operation Bernau. The 8th Destroyer Flotilla (Kapitän zur See Erdmenger) and made up of *Z23*, *Z24*, *Z27*, *Z32*, *Z37* and the ex-Royal Netherlands Navy's *ZH1* (formerly *Gerard Callenburgh*), together with a half dozen torpedo boats, put to sea from the Gironde. The next day this force meet the *Osorno* and escorted her safely into port, beating off vigorous attacks by the RAF's Coastal Command on the way home. Unfortunately for Germany's industry, the *Osorno* hit a wreck in the estuary and had to be beached to save the cargo.

Obviously, the Royal Navy was not going to allow this to happen too often! On December 26, when a similar operation, code-named *Trave*, was attempted, the British were waiting. The *Enterprise*, a Royal Canadian Navy cruiser, and HMS *Glasgow*, chased the blockade runner, *Alsterufer*, together with a covering force which included a Free French destroyer. The *Alsterufer* was sunk whilst still far out at sea by a very long range Liberator bomber. The German destroyer force were at sea by this time and were hastily recalled. The Allied force managed to intercept the destroyers and engaged them, although the latter were superior in numbers. This small action left the destroyer *Z27* (with Erdmenger aboard) and two torpedo boats sinking, without loss to the Allies. The Biscayan swell had severely hampered the seahandling of the destroyers and resulted in little or no manoeuvring room.

In 1944, both destroyers and their smaller contemporaries, torpedo boats, tried to interfere with the Allied landings in Normandy, but, by this time, they were totally out-classed and outnumbered – they could do little to stop or hinder the inevitable, even though a determined night action was fought. Slowly, the advancing Allied armies made the tenure of the occupied ports, especially in Brittany, impossible. Ushant was the grave of Z32 which was driven ashore by the gallant Canadian destroyers Haida and Huron. Le Havre, for so long the home of destroyers and torpedo boats, was evacuated in August, but not without loss. Z23 was caught off La Palice and scuttled after being crippled by RAF bombers. Rocket-carrying fighter-bombers sank Z24 and T24 off Le Verdan, whilst Bordeaux was the final resting place of Z37 (a 1936A (Mob) type destroyer) in company with several auxiliary patrol ships and minesweepers.

The same year saw the re-emergence of a destroyer presence in the Baltic when the 6th Flotilla arrived to attempt to prevent Soviet domination by a concerted mining task. The commander of these operations was Kapitän zur See Peters, the former skipper of Z25. Torpedo boats were also operational in this theatre, T18 and T31 falling victim to Russian forces in 1944. On December 12 1944 both Z35 and Z36 were mined in the Gulf of Finland. The writing was on the wall for the Kriegsmarine.

Passing mention has been made above of the torpedo boat, a type which has now passed out of the naval scene. After Versailles, a dozen torpedo boats, plus four reserves, were all that was left of the proud torpedo boat force of World War 1. Germany started World War 2 with 11 of the larger type, launched between 1926 and 1928. These boats were designed with the expertise of the 1914–18 conflict, but they still lacked sufficient freeboard to make them good weather boats. A characteristic design feature was the tall fore-funnel and small, squat bridge. Later designs had a less powerful armament but more torpedo tubes. The latter were rarely used as the type was employed in the escort role. The 1,750 tons Elbing Class (1939 type T22–T36) were as well armed as many destroyers and they were often deployed as such. The older boats, mainly built before World War 1, were used for training and as gunnery tenders.

Torpedo boats were operated under the auspices of the Flag Officer, Torpedo boats (Führer der Torpedoboote or FdT), until the major shake-up of the operational commands in 1942. Until this time, the FdT had also been in charge of E-boats and destroyers. The new structure meant that torpedo boats then came under the command of the FdZ, in effect a complete reversal! E-boats were transferred to their own Flag Officer.

To the Germans, the T-boat was virtually a small destroyer, armed with torpedoes to engage the capital ships of an opposing battle fleet. World War 2 did not witness any such confrontation and so saw the torpedo boats used as minelayers, transports and escorts.

When the war began, Germany's dozen large torpedo boats had already been reduced to 11 by the accidental sinking of Tiger in the Baltic during 'war games' with destroyers. The 1,320 tons T-boat collided with Z3 Max Schultze – to be sunk in the North Sea six months later. When the invasion of Poland began on September 1 1939, the FdT, Konter-Admiral Lütjens, was aboard a destroyer leading the seaborne offensive in the Baltic, but within three days (and Britain's declaration of war) he was in the North Sea with the cream of his destroyer forces together with the 5th and 6th Torpedo boat Flotillas. These units were commanded by Korvetten-Kapitän Heyke and Korvetten-Kapitän Wane respectively, and consisted of the 1923 type and 1924 type torpedo boats, originally classed as destroyers. These vessels, under the total control of Vize-Admiral Deusch, were engaged in the laying of the Westwall mine barrage whilst covered by four cruisers and the destroyers.

Meanwhile in the Baltic, the somewhat ancient torpedo boat T196 (launched in April 1911) shelled Polish ports in company with the old battleship Schleswig-Holstein. This was the beginning of a war-long presence in the eastern Baltic by torpedo boats, engaged mainly in security patrols. During the first year of the war, several operations were mounted with the assistance of T-boats, but the next major operation was the invasion of Denmark and Norway.

Torpedo boats were used in the attacks on southern Norway, escorting large warships and acting as transports. Their targets were Bergen, Kristiansand, Arendal and Oslofjord. Again units of this force were destined to remain in the Norwegian theatre throughout the war, but there was a casualty or two. Albatros, built in the early 1920s under the terms of Versailles, was sunk by the Norwegian minelayer Olav Tryggvason in Oslofjord. The Skagerrak, between Norway and Denmark, was the scene of the loss of Leopard after a collision with the minelayer Preussen.

Most of the other torpedo boats involved survived until the destruction from the air of so many German surface warships in 1944.

The German war machine moved ever onward and soon the Low Countries and France were crushed beneath the jackboot. These countries provided a rich harvest of warships which were impressed into service with the Kriegsmarine. In 1943, following the surrender of Italy to the Allies, Italian torpedo boats were also to be found under the German flag. During the last two years of World War 2, two all-captured torpedo boat flotillas were operational using French, Italian and Yugoslavian boats of varying ages, dimensions and operational fitness. All these units helped, of course, to provide the Kriegsmarine with auxiliary vessels for mining operations and escort. In the Mediterranean, there was the equally important task of patrolling the islands and creeks from which anti-Nazi partisans operated.

Before the war, torpedo boats looking somewhat alike, they were marked with identifying initials on their bows rather like the pennant numbers of the Royal Navy or the hull numbers of the United States Navy. For example, 1923 type *Greif* was marked GR and the later 1924 type, *Leopard* was marked LP. Pre-war, the destroyers of the Kriegsmarine also carried hull marks, but in their case they used hull numbers to indicate the warship's position in the Zerstörer-flotilla not her Z-number. Thus it is not particularly sensible to use this method to identify the warships. The organisation of the destroyer and torpedo forces was not hard and fast in any case because warships could be allocated to the command of task force commanders. After the war both destroyers and torpedoes were allocated to the victorious navies, even the Royal Navy, which received *Z38*. She went on to serve as HMS *Nonsuch* until 1949. Russia seems to have received by far the most of appropriated warships, especially torpedo boats, including one of the successful Elbing Class – *T33* which became *Primierny* in 1946.

During the war, a dozen T-boats were ordered from Dutch yards, but none saw action. This was perhaps unfortunate for the Kriegsmarine because their displacement of 2,500 tons and four 137 mm guns would have made them formidable destroyers.

Up until now, this introduction has dwelt on the destroyer forces – the offensive forces, and has not mentioned the workhorses of many a seaborne operation – the minesweepers. Although under the command of a Flag Officer (Führer der Minensuchboote or FdM), these warships were allocated to the Security Forces of the Kriegsmarine, rather than the Reconnaissance Forces like destroyers and torpedo boats. When the war broke out the flagship of the FdM (Kapitän zur See Ruge) was the torpedo boat *T196*, already mentioned.

Minesweepers (Minensuchboote) together with their counterparts, minelayers (Minenlegere or Minenschiffe) were not rated very highly when the terms of the Treaty of Versailles was drawn up and hence were lumped together with the auxiliary and ancillary craft.

Large numbers of both craft were deployed during World War 2, including during the first years at least, several former Kaiserliche Marine types, but these vessels were a well-tried design and had been employed in the early inter-war mine clearing operations. Many were given new roles, such as tenders to R-boats and experimental craft. A few even survived to be impressed into United States Navy service as targets in 1945-6.

In 1935, a new design appeared, still largely based on designs used 20 years before, but oil-burning instead of steam-propelled. However, in 1940, another design, with more powerful anti-aircraft defences, was initiated. The first of these craft, launched in 1942, was again steam-powered, showing that Germany had already begun to worry about oil supplies. Yet another design appeared in 1944 (the 1943 type) which was a multi-purpose minesweeper, minelayer, escort and also used as a torpedo recovery vessel.

The small minesweeper types, such as the Raümboote have been dealt with in the companion volume *E-Boats and Coastal Craft*, so this account is limited to the vessels which made up the 30 or so minesweeper flotillas, whose numbers were in the M-series.

Although history seems to have chosen to highlight the more glamorous naval details of World War 2, the minesweepers were in at the start, and many out-served the mighty capital ships, being involved in the post-war operations to clear the thousands of mines sown during the hostilities. The minesweepers' war began in Poland, when the 1st Minesweeper Flotilla swept a channel for the advancing German naval forces. The first casualty was apparently *M85* which ran on to a Polish submarine-laid mine barrage north of Heisterment on October 1 1939. *M85* (not to be confused with the 1935 type of the same number) was an Emden-built World War 1 type of 690 tons.

Like many other available German warships, minesweepers played their part in the invasion of Denmark and Norway in April 1940, led by the newly-promoted Kommodore Ruge. Two smaller minesweepers were lost to Allied submarine attacks, but a few days later the diesel-powered *M6* sank the British submarine *Tarpon* with depth charges. Other minesweepers were lost trying to clear submarine-laid mines so that German transports could bring in the invasion forces, but all in all the sweepers gave a good account of themselves.

In 1942, with the tide of the war beginning to turn against the Germans, minesweepers and minelayers were engaged in operations off the North and Polar coasts of Norway to lay defensive mine barrages against Soviet submarine attacks. In these actions, the minelayer *Brummer* (formerly the Royal Norwegian ship *Olav Tryggvasan*) was the dominant vessel and several times was nearly the victor over Soviet submarines which tried to interfere with the minelaying. *Brummer* survived her mission in these waters only to be sunk at Kiel after an air attack in 1945. The warships taking part in these operations were grouped under the command of Kapitän zur See Schönermark and were termed Group Nord.

In 1942, German minesweepers in the Gulf of Finland were able to assist their tacit allies, Finland, when Soviet naval forces attacked Someri. *M18* and *M37* used their 105 mm and 37 mm guns to good advantage against the Soviet troops and landing craft. Here too, the tide was turning against the Axis.

Minesweeper escort operations in the English Channel and Bay of Biscay were not without risk, especially as the Allies were slowly gaining air superiority over the coastal areas of 'Fortress Europe'. British Coastal Forces took their toll of the sweepers, such as *M8*, attacked and sunk off the Hook of Holland in May 1943 and *M153*, destroyed by gunfire in July of the same year. It was 1944, however, when anti-convoy sweeps by both aircraft and warships led to heavy losses by the Kriegsmarine. The Channel coasts of France and the Low Countries were the best hunting grounds for the Allies. The pre-D-Day build up in the Channel led to the successful Operation Channel Stop by Albacores and Avengers of the Royal Navy and Beaufighters of the RAF when all types of German shipping were attacked whenever they ventured forth.

After D-Day many escorts which could not be fought out of naval harbours were scuttled by their crews. Many such wrecks had to be raised in order to open the ports for normal traffic after the war and several smaller warships were salvaged for further service. Several minesweepers were converted to commercial hulls and one was even in service with the Bundesmarine (Federal German Navy) until 1963.

Although Kriegsmarine escorts did not have to participate in major convoy and task forces on an oceanic scale, the sheer volume of coastal convoy traffic was tremendous. In the early war years, destroyers and torpedo boats were often to be found escorting one or more capital ships and played a major part in the success of several operations, such as the transfer of the powerful battleship *Tirpitz* to Norway, and the infamous Channel Dash. The main hunting grounds of the destroyers were in northern climes such as the Baltic, Skagerrak and North Sea. Undoubtedly, it is Narvik which will be the main theatre of operations which posterity will associate with the Zerstörer!

The photographs in this book have been selected with care from the Bundesarchiv, Koblenz (the approximate German equivalent of the US National Archives or the British Public Records Office). Particular attention has been devoted to choosing photographs which will be fresh to the majority of readers, although it is inevitable that one or two may be familiar. Other than this, the author's prime concern has been to choose good-quality photographs which illustrate the type of detail that enthusiasts and modellers require. In certain instances quality has, to a degree, been sacrificed in order to include a particularly interesting photograph. For the most part, however, the quality speaks for itself.

The Bundesarchiv files hold some one million black and white negatives of Wehrmacht and Luftwaffe subjects, including 150,000 on the Kriegsmarine, some 20,000 glass negatives from the inter-war period and several hundred colour photographs. Sheer numbers is one of the problems which makes the compilation of a book such as this difficult. Other difficulties include the fact that, in the vast majority of cases, the negatives have not been printed so the researcher is forced to look through box after box of 35 mm contact strips – some 250 boxes containing an average of over 5,000 pictures each, plus folders containing a further 115,000 contact prints of the Waffen-SS; moreover, cataloguing and indexing the negatives is neither an easy nor a short task, with the result that, at the present time, Luftwaffe and Wehrmacht subjects as well as entirely separate theatres of operations are intermingled in the same files.

There is a simple explanation for this confusion. The Bundesarchiv photographs were taken by war correspondents attached to German military units, and the negatives were originally stored in the Reich Propaganda Ministry in Berlin. Towards the close of World War 2, all the photographs – then numbering some $3\frac{1}{2}$ million – were ordered to be destroyed. One man in the Ministry, a Herr Evers, realised that they should be preserved for posterity and, acting entirely unofficially and on his own initiative, commandeered the first available suitable transport – two refrigerated fish trucks – loaded the negatives into them, and set out for safety. Unfortunately, one of the trucks disappeared en route and, to this day, nobody knows what happened to it. The remainder were captured by the Americans and shipped to Washington, where they remained for 20 years before the majority were returned to the government of West Germany. A large number, however, still reside in Washington. Thus the Bundesarchiv files are incomplete, with infuriating gaps for any researcher. Specifically, they end in the autumn of 1944, after Arnhem, and thus record none of the drama of the closing months of the war.

The photographs are currently housed in a modern office block in Koblenz, overlooking the River Mosel. The priceless negatives are stored in the basement, and there are strict security checks on anyone seeking admission to the Bildarchiv (Photo Archive). Regretably, and the author has been asked to stress this point, the archives are *only open to bona fide authors and publishers, and prints can only be supplied for reproduction in a book or magazine.* They CANNOT be supplied to private collectors or enthusiasts for personal use, so *please* – don't write to the Bundesarchiv or the publishers of this book asking for copy prints, because they cannot be provided. The well-equipped photo laboratory at the Bundesarchiv is only capable of handling some 80 to 100 prints per day because each is printed individually under strictly controlled conditions – another reason for the fine quality of the photographs but also a contributory factor in the above legislation.

THE PHOTOGRAPHS

Above Speeding along in the screen of a battlegroup moving towards the Norwegian coast, a *Z1—Z16* Class destroyer shows off a fine turn of speed; the class was credited with 38 knots (MN/1623/21a).

Left Details of the bow and foremast of *Brummer*, a captured minelayer (113MW/5630/6).

Below A familiar sight on the decks of most escorts was the anti-submarine depth charge. These particular examples are being examined here by an able-seaman (Matrosen-Gefreiter) and a deck-hand (Bootsmann) (MN/1381/12a).

Above Dressed in working rig and oil-skins, this deck party practises 'good housekeeping' aboard a destroyer in Norwegian waters (MN/1433/20a).

Below Light anti-aircraft guns, positioned on the after-funnel gun sponson of a large destroyer. Note the ready-use ammunition lockers around the position—later in the war, with bitter experience, these lockers were replaced with splinter matting (MN/1433/35a).

Above This photograph of a destroyer's officers' mess given an indication of the space available in this type of warship. The tunics being worn in this photograph are the standard Kriegsmarine summer pattern (MN/1579/2a).

Below The superstructure of a 1934-type destroyer steaming at defence stations. Of interest in this shot are the searchlight and range-finder positions (MN/1628/37a).

Above Displaying one of the more distinctive disruptive camouflage patterns to be used on war-time German destroyers is *Z4 Richard Beitzen* when photographed off Norway in 1941 (MN/2017/39).

Left Following in the wake of the heavy cruiser *Prinz Eugen* is thought to be *Z4 Richard Beitzen*, part of the screening force for the famous Channel Dash in 1942 (14MO/683/24).

Below The famous leader of the 8th Destroyer Flotilla—Flotilla Narvik—from March to December 1943, was Kapitän zur See Hans Erdmenger. The Korvetten-Kapitän to Erdmenger's right is wearing, incidentally, the War Order of the German Cross under the eagle badge, whilst the 'boss' wears the Destroyer Badge beneath the breast Iron Cross (262/1522/3a).

Above left A three-quarters view of *Narvik* Class destroyer *Z24*, a real beauty and capable of 38.5 knots. This photograph appears to have been taken after the 1942–3 refit of the class, when the 15 cm twin turret was fitted (just visible in front of the superstructure) (262/1522/6a).

Left Another camouflage variation on a 1936B type destroyer taken before the refitting of the main armament. This particular ship is thought to be *Z26*, which was sunk by *HMS Trinidad* in March 1942 and so did not receive the C38 mounting (74aMW/3696/3).

Above An interesting shot of the range-finder crew in action at their position aft of the second funnel (95/MW/4741/26).

Right A view from the superstructure of the deck of the speeding destroyer, *Z8 Bruno Heinemann* which shows the heavy 3.7 cm flak mounting in the foreground and a 15 cm mounting aft (96/MW/4755/20a).

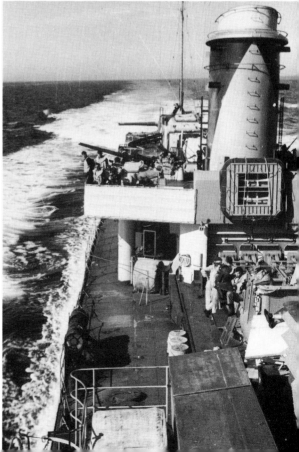

Left The traditional armament of a destroyer was always the torpedo. In this photo, the two banks of tubes can be seen swung out for action; in the foreground is the 'back' end of the forward tubes, and underneath the 3.7 cm sponson is the 'business' end of the after bank (108/MW/5363/13a).

Below On passage down the Channel during *Operation Cerberus*, destroyers of the 5th Flotilla escort the battlecruiser *Gneisenau* home to Kiel. Note the depth charges lashed to the railings (108/MW/5636/14a).

Right An unusual view of the underwater hull of a 1936A type destroyer in dry dock, complete with clipper stem. This latter feature was designed to provide more buoyancy in heavy weather than the traditional straight stem (103/MW/5109/33).

Above Moving through the ice is one of the 1934 type destroyers built in 1935–7 as an attempt to offset the quantity of Allied destroyers by quality. Unfortunately, the class were notoriously bad seakeepers and so did not provide that much sought after superiority (112/MW/5551/34).

Below An evocative shot of a *Z17—Z22* destroyer 'creaming' past a larger warship (112MW/5555/16).

Above Norway became a major theatre of operations for the Kriegsmarine's destroyer force; it was also the graveyard for some dozen units. Many of the actions were in association with capital ships and this photograph was taken from *Admiral Hipper* in April 1940 (113MW/5604/37a).

Below In April 1940, the fjords around the Norwegian port of Narvik were to see the destruction of ten destroyers during the two famous Battles of Narvik. As a result of these losses, the German destroyer force was radically reorganised (113/MW/5604/38a).

Inset Some 14 destroyers were involved in the German invasion of Denmark and Norway—Operation Weserübung—in 1940. This is *Z16 Friedrich Eckoldt* (113MW/5603/13a).

Background photograph Escorting a 'big boy' in polar waters is an early destroyer with two single 12.7 cm mountings forward (112MW/5558/27).

Above left 1934A type destroyers alongside. This early type was constructed in clear defiance of the Treaty of Versailles and six of the 16 built survived the war. These are units of the 2nd Flotilla at Cuxhaven in April 1940 (113MW/5607/3).

Far left The forward battery of 12.7 cm guns, with the eagle-decorated bridge behind, of the former Norwegian minelayer *Brummer* (113MW/5630/11).

Left With signal flags flying, a flotilla off Trondheim in July 1940, taken from *Z20*. Note the use of the German National Flag as an aircraft recognition marking on the deck (114MW/5698/3a).

Above Putting to sea as escort for a capital ship sortie, possibly with the *Scharnhorst*, an early destroyer of the *Leberecht Maas* Class shows off its sleek lines (114MW/5668/9).

Right The Command Flag, just visible on the foremast of *Z15 Erich Steinbrinck*, indicates the presence of the flotilla Commander, Fregatten-Kapitän Berger. The destroyer appears to be passing through the Kiel Canal and the date is sometime in August 1940 (115MW/5739/3a).

Overleaf The flotilla moves into position to screen a departing capital ship—probably a heavy cruiser. The nearer warship is *Z14 Friedrich Ihn* (115MW/5741/3a).

Above left Complete with mines and sweeping gear on the quarter deck this destroyer (*Z10 Hans Lerdy*) shows the narrow beam and raked stern of her type. The shot was taken from the larger *Z20* (115MW/5742/18).

Far left General-Admiral Karl Dönitz, with other officers (including a Kapitän zur See and a Korvetten-Kapitän) leave a destroyer by Admiral's barge. (115MW/5743/15a).

Left These two matelots are busy with a home brew kit—their style of dress is noteworthy (MW/6868/17).

Above What a dazzler! The identity of this unusually marked destroyer is, unfortunately, obscure, but it could be the captured Royal Netherlands Navy destroyer, *ZH1*. Equally obscure are the colours of the 'splinter' scheme (MW/6766/6).

Right The early destroyer designs were rather 'damp' ships even in moderate seas, as this photograph shows. Note the minerails running parallel to the ship's side (MW/6871/7).

Above The skipper. An escort's commanding officer, wrapped up against the elements and wearing a life preserver, rests against the open bridge's magnetic compass repeater (MW/6872/23a).

Left Destroyers, spending their first winter at war, are huddled together in a German naval port (112MW/5559/4).

Right Moving alongside a sister-ship is the 1936A type destroyer *Z24* of the 8th Flotilla (Kapitän zur See Pönitz). This photograph was taken off the French coast in the summer of 1941; three years later *Z24* was to be sunk by aircraft rocket fire off the same country's coast (103MW/5101/6).

Above left A torpedo boat flotilla in harbour and photographed shortly before the outbreak of war. The destroyer-size warship in the background is the 1924 type torpedo boat, *Jaguar*, which was launched in 1928 (108/MW/5357/12a).

Left This three-quarter view of a 1924 type *T-Boot* shows the lack of freeboard which caused problems when the vessel had to sail through rough weather (111/MW/5505/14).

Above The warlike appearance of this torpedo boat, of the *T22—T36* Class, includes an angular camouflage scheme and gear over and above the peacetime fit, for example the life-raft on 'A' turret (MN1380/10a).

Right Alongside what appears to be a lock on the Kiel Canal are two torpedo boats and several smaller craft. The low, squat appearance of the forward superstructure and the fairly tall funnels of the *T-Boot* show up well here (111/MW/5505/16).

Above left Speeding towards an objective in Norway is a flotilla of a torpedo-boats carrying German Alpine troops, wrapped in bulky life jackets (MS/985/6a).

Above right The troops were transferred to impressed local craft to be ferried ashore (MS/985/16a).

Below Armed with three 10.5 cm guns and assorted 2 cm automatic light flak guns, besides the traditional banks of torpedo tubes, the early torpedo boats were originally rated as destroyers (MN/1027/20a).

Above Capable of 35 knots, the 1937 type torpedo boats were powerful enough to act as escorts when it became clear that their intended role in a fleet-to-fleet engagement would not be forthcoming (MW/6871/25).

Below Although better armed than their predecessors, the 1937 type torpedo boats had their anti-aircraft armament augmented with light flak guns after war experience. To save top weight, a bank of torpedo-tubes was removed thus allowing the fitting of the extra guns (MW/6872/30a).

Above The cramped decks of two torpedo boats alongside—note the U-boat pens in the background. The warship on the left is a 1937 type, whilst the vessel on the right is an example of the older 1935 type (MW/6873/21).

Below Seen over the quarter deck of a sister-ship is a lozenge camouflaged torpedo-boat (MW/6840/24a).

Above This particular shot is interesting because it shows both camouflaged and non-camouflaged torpedo boats. To the left, a quadruple 2 cm flak-vierling installation probably indicates that that particular T-Boat has just been completed (MW/6874/24).

Below The flotilla at sea—the silhouettes of both 1935 and 1937 types (MW/6830/32).

Flotilla manoeuvres:

Left Changing formation, the 1935 type shows off its port side camouflage. The quadruple 2 cm mounting, as well as the crew, are depicted in useful detail for the modeller (MW/ 6837/20a).

Above A 1935 type torpedo boat leads a radar-equipped and larger 1937 type (MW/6837/ 19a).

Right This warship has a rather alarming angle of heel as it crosses the wake of another (MW/6679/22a).

Above One of several veterans of the World War 1 torpedo boat forces to serve in the 1939–45 conflict was *T151*, seen here before being converted for service as a torpedo recovery vessel and renamed *Komet*. She survived the war and was scrapped in the Netherlands 42 years after she first touched the water in 1907 (109MW/5421/2a).

Left This is thought to be the impressed Italian torpedo boat *Goanadiere* on a sortie with a German crew in the Mediterranean (MS/985/4a).

Facing page Two views of captured and interned Danish torpedo boats, guarded by a cutlass-bearing sailor. The ship's name, *Dragon*, appears on the emergency steering position's screen on the nearest boat (MN/1031/29a and 30a).

Left Caricatures painted on a 15 cm gun turret—the one on the right is obviously Stalin, and the others are intended to look like Churchill and Roosevelt. Looking on (right) is an Iron Cross-decorated Chief Petty Officer (Obermaat) (74aMW/3693/24a).

Below left The forward gun crew of a torpedo boat. The large, rectangular radar aerials show up well in this view (MW/6871/24).

Right A photograph taken alongside the port side of a destroyer showing the local torpedo-tube control position (foreground), the main battery rangefinder (above) and one of the 3.7 cm flak mountings (middle ground) (108MW/5363/51).

Below A peaceful scene, probably a Sunday at sea—note the rather unorthodox use of the life-rafts! (MN/1630/28a).

Left In the foreground of this picture, an administration Leutnant zur See (right) chats to an engineering Kapitän-Leutnant. The individual 'trades' of these officers can be seen immediately above their respective sleeve insignia (MN/1380/36a).

Below Torpedo firing practice aboard a Kriegsmarine destroyer. On the left is the communications number and on the right (wearing a flying helmet?!) is the firing crewman (108MW/5363/9a).

Right A torpedo engineer (Torpedomechaniker) supervises the loading of an 'eel' into a tube aboard a destroyer (MN/1433/14a).

Below right Large and difficult to handle though they were, torpedoes needed regular maintenance. Note the highly polished finish of the propellers and rudders (MN/2798/35).

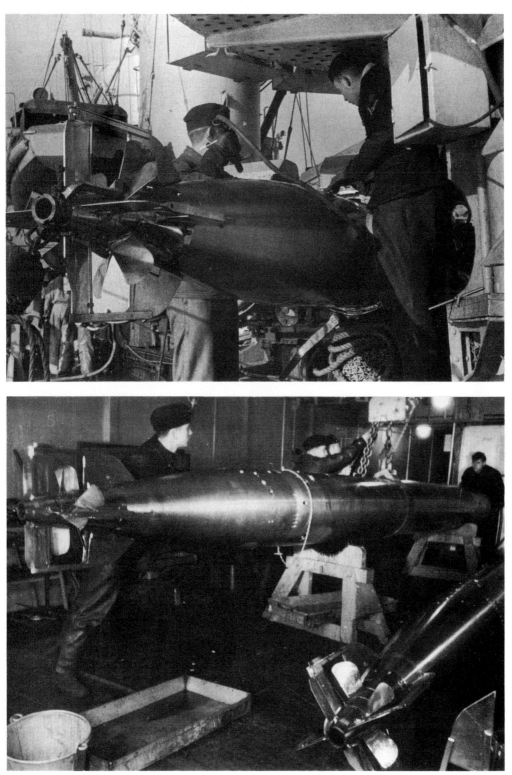

Above The crew of a 3.7 cm gun closed up for a practice shoot. In the foreground, a Matrose holds one of the shells (57MW/2823/8a).

Left Watching the fall of shot is a leading seaman (Matrosen-Gefreiter) with the binoculars, a communications rating and a petty officer (Maat) (111MW/5503/35).

Above right A hit! This torpedo boat's port 3.7 cm gun crew rejoice at their skill—or luck. Not all the crew are wearing steel helmets, the missing ones can be seen in racks on the bridge screen above (74aMW/3696/27a).

Right A successful action by destroyers or torpedo boats? We shall probably never know (75MW/ 3717/71).

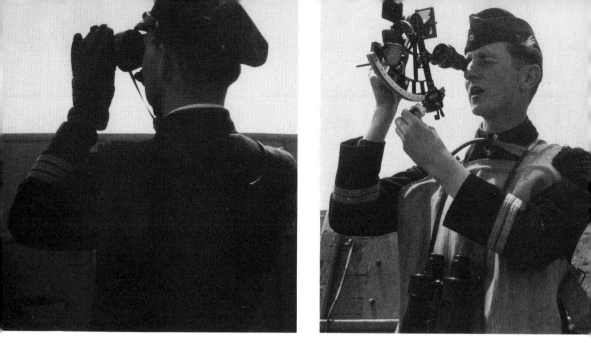

Above left Command of Kriegsmarine destroyers was frequently given to a three-ringer, a Korvetten-Kapitän, whilst command of the flotilla was usually in the hands of a Kapitän zur See (96MW/4755/25a).

Above right The noon sun sight is taken by an Oberleutnant zur See (129MW/6419/32).

Below A torpedo boat in refit. Amongst the mass of cables it is possible to determine the trunking and associated pipes of the funnel which characterised the 1935 type boats (112MW/5582/26).

Above A torpedo boat's skipper ponders the chart as a Leutnant zur See looks on. The unofficial uniform jacket is not as unusual as may be thought—at sea it was always possible to escape the rigid rules of dress (115MW/5848/12).

Below Keeping a sharp look out on *Z8 Bruno Heinemann* are an Oberleutnant zur See (left) and a capless Kapitän-Leutnant (96MW/4755/27a).

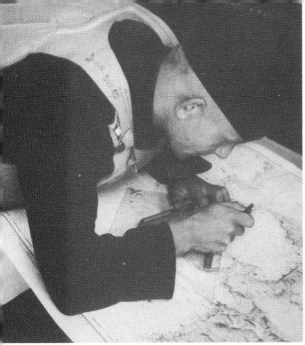

Above far left An accurate position was most important to the boat's well being in coastal waters which may have been mined (95MW/4741/30).

Above left The flotilla's senior officer on the bridge wearing another variation in the standard dress of the day—a battledress jacket. Unfortunately, the Kapitän zur See's identity remains unknown (MW/6839/5).

Left Expecting heavy weather, the bridge crew look expectantly over the starboard wing's screen (MW/6873/31).

Above Ah ha! They've seen something. The rather bulky lifejackets must have caused problems in the cramped conditions of a small warship, especially in excitement (MW/6873/34).

Below Meanwhile on the port bridge-wing, the Captain reassures his men. Note the 2 cm flak gun in the left foreground (MW/6873/32).

Left Cruising stations aboard a 1937 type torpedo boat which appears to be on convoy-escort duty (MW/6871/29).

Below left The starboard side of a speeding T-boat with its naval ensign worn at the gaff. This photograph comes from a series of shots of escorts for the cruiser *Lützow* in northern waters (MN/1025/4).

Right A participant in the defence of Dieppe, this warship displays both aircraft and submarine kills. Of special interest is the splinter matting and the Viking-ship emblem on the mast (102MW/5070/11a).

Below The German naval ensign at the gaff of a Kriegsmarine escort. This flag was introduced in November 1935, the same year as the German Navy changed its name from Reichsmarine (M4/K3K17/832/11a).

Left Two examples of different officer headgear; on the left, the peaked cap of a senior officer and the forage cap of a more junior one (129MW/ 6419/10).

Below Getting a breath of fresh air, adjacent to part of his charge is a mine engineer (Sperr-mechaniker). The mine-carrying rails at his feet are within the care of his trade (MW/1628/36a).

Right Gently does it. Mines being transferred from a supply vessel to the destroyer, *Z12 Erich Giese*. The ship's name is worn by several of the deck ratings on their cap tallies (MN/1584/15a).

Below right and overleaf German warships were very successful in their mining operations at the beginning of the war and here a *T13* Class torpedo boat stocks up with the tethered variety ready for another sortie (104aMW/5195/16a and 25a).

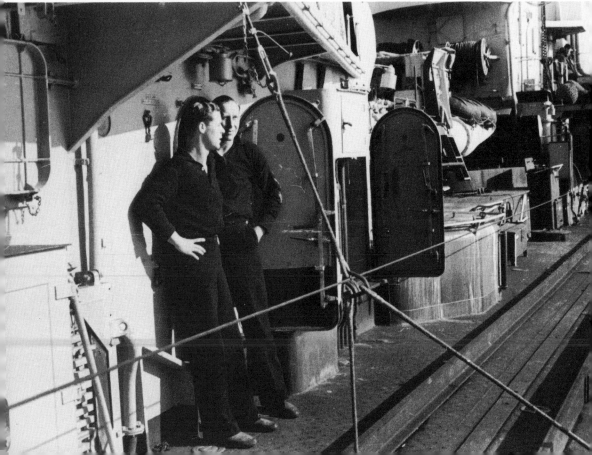

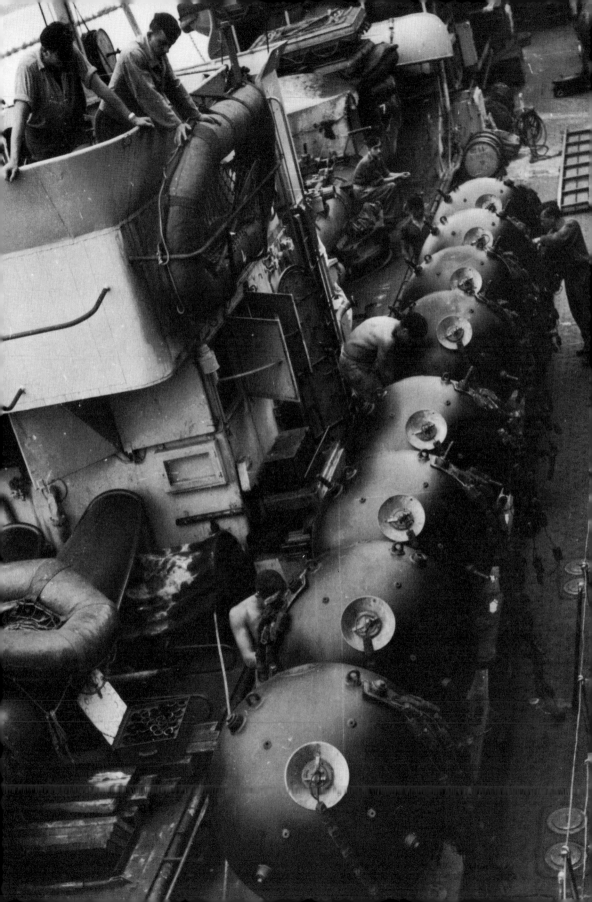

Right Moving at speed, a 1935 type minesweeper crosses the wake of another warship. This type, powered by oil-fired engines, was well fitted to escort tasks as well as its intended role (57MW/2823/25a).

Below A 1935 type mine-sweeper (Minensuchboot) flotilla leaves port in a flurry of semaphore signals (99aMW/4945/24a).

Above Relaxing on the sweep deck, a group of officers try the local brew. The Oberleutnant zur See on the left wears the Iron Cross First Class on his breast whilst the Leutnant zur See (right) is actually an artillery/gunnery specialist (MW/6668/37a).

Below Framed by the after 10.5 cm gun of a sister-ship, this *M25* Class minesweeper demonstrates its remarkable manoeuvrability (99aMW/4945/35a).

Above Sister-ships these, yet they have totally different camouflage schemes. What a pity this is not a colour shot! (MN/1396/3a).

Below left Laying off the Baltic coast, this minesweeper awaits the liberty boat and a spot of shore leave. Note the command pennant at the masthead (MW/6668/24a).

Below right Could this be an escort for a German blockade runner? Besides the two minesweepers, it is possible to make out the silhouette of an Arado 196 floatplane in the distance (MW/6672/9a).

Background photograph Armed with two 10.5 cm, two 3.7 cm and six 2 cm guns, the 1935 type minesweeper was a useful escort to other ships, or in flotilla operations with its own kind. (MW/6679/14a).

Inset below They were frequently in action off the coasts of occupied Europe (57MW/2823/20a).

Inset below right A flotilla at sea—note the characteristic seaboat davit (amidships) of this type (99aMW/4945/35a).

Left The 10.5 cm mounting was particularly suited to a dual-purpose role, although its poor protection made it unpleasant to man in extreme climates, such as the polar coast of Norway (99aMW/4946/24).

Below Threading their way through the ice floes of the Norwegian Sea, two of the old fashioned, coal-burning minesweepers patrol the sea-lanes (112MW/5558/28).

Bottom Auxiliary minesweepers were often ex-mercantile vessels and frequently they were used to detonate mines. Perhaps this vessel did just that (101aMW/5037/29a).

Right Tools of the trade . . . the sweep gear stowed but ready for action once the minesweeper is at sea, makes a good place to grab a few moments' relaxation (129MW/6403/8).

Below right Good housekeeping is as important in war as it is in peace. This minesweeper's hull is getting a once-over before the 'splinter' type camouflage is applied (108MW/5358/34a).

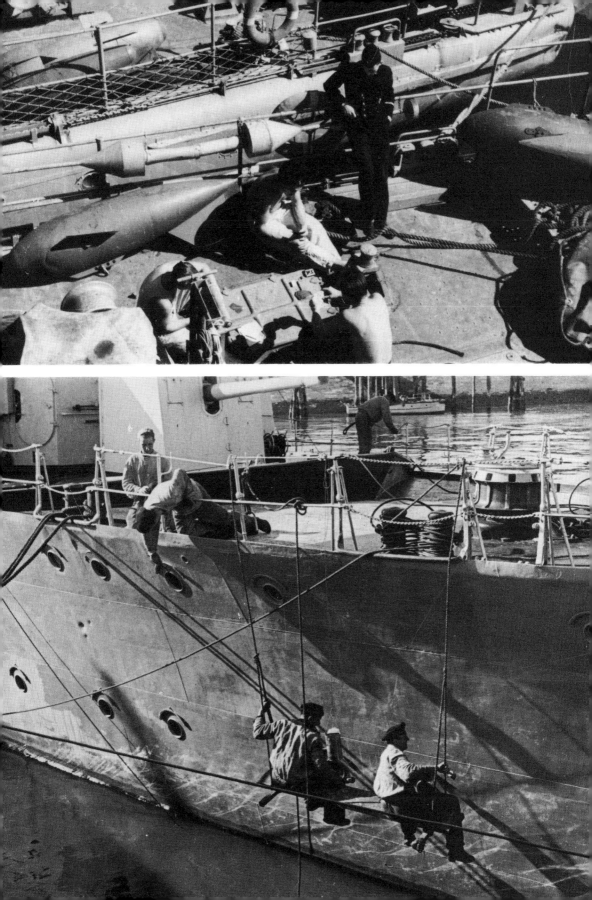

68

Above left Preparing the gear on the sweep deck for the water (95MW/4741/8).

Left Retrieving the gear was difficult enough in calm seas but just imagine the hazards involved when a sea was running. The unofficial shirt is interesting, but not unusual; note also the Petty Officer's rating anchor displayed on the nearest man's tunic (104aMW/5177/16a).

Above When mines of the tethered variety were swept, they came to the surface under their own buoyancy and were detonated there by small arms fire from the minesweeper, as this photograph shows. The officer, by his shoulder strap, is a Kapitän-Leutnant (113MW/5623/16a).

Below This view through a periscope or range-finder shows the fast fleet sloop *F8* at speed. This warship, one of a class of ten, was built by Blohm und Voss and survived the war to be scrapped in 1950 (108MW/5358/7a).

Above Such steamers as this were used in a variety of roles, such as auxiliary transports and accommodation ships. In 1945, any vessels afloat in the Baltic were used to evacuate refugees in a bid to escape the advancing Soviets (111MW/5546/27a).

Left Alert crewmen aboard an unidentified vessel (108MW/5363/11a).

Above right Many of the smaller German warships were coal-fired and this was a grimy, backbreaking job for the stokers (129MW/6439/30a).

Right The machinery space of a German escort—the engine room telegraph appears to indicate 'full ahead' (129MW/6441/14a).

Far right The footplate of a destroyer with its heavily lagged steam pipes (99aMW/4945/17a).

Above No, not a record cutting machine, but more probably an anti-submarine 'sonar' locating device (99a/MW/4945/19a).

Left Manning a range-finder on a destroyer's bridge was this sailor's action station (96MW/4755/29a).

Above right The communications ratings close up on a torpedo boat (MW/6872/8a).

Right The after end of a minesweeper's superstructure showing part of the 10.5 cm main armament (MW/6679/30a).

Above A 2 cm anti-aircraft crew on a Kriegsmarine escort vessel (101aMW/5030/19).

Below Another crew carry out light maintenance on their charge (101aMW/5042/17a).

Right Anti-aircraft mountings on an auxiliary minesweeper (Sperrbrecher) trained for action (129MW/6436/18).

Above Another light gun mounting aboard an escort manned by a leading seaman in the gunnery branch (right). The gunnery trade badge (crossed cannons) is worn above the double rank chevrons (MW/6872/9a).

Below A five-man crew of a dual-purpose 2 cm mounting in action (129MW/6437/36).

Above right A gun crew's communicator; of interest are the eagle emblem on the forage cap and the cornflower blue collar patch of a rating (129MW/6419/38).

Above far right The three forms of tactical communications are shown in this photograph; a signaller using semaphore, to his left a small signal lamp, and stowed below the halyards are signal flags (MW/6668/37a).

Right Time for lunch. The sweep-deck crew relax with a potato stew. The man on the right wears, from the top, the trade badge of a deck rating, a leading seaman's chevrons and the trade badge of an artillery gunner (MW/6871/27).

Above A seaboat, carrying in the bow an officer and two Chief Petty Officer yeomen (Schreiberobermaate) (111MW/5503/32).

Left This is probably an impressed Swedish steamer, but more interesting is the senior leading seaman (Matrosenhauptgefreiter) in the signal branch of the Kriegsmarine (112MW/5551/24).

Above right keeping a sharp look-out on a minesweeper. Note the bridge fittings (95MW/4741/32).

Right A gun crew relaxes with the small ship's mascot (and probably a useful emergency food supply). The man, second from the right, is wearing the 'Edelweiss' emblem more usually associated with U-boats (115MW/5737/13).

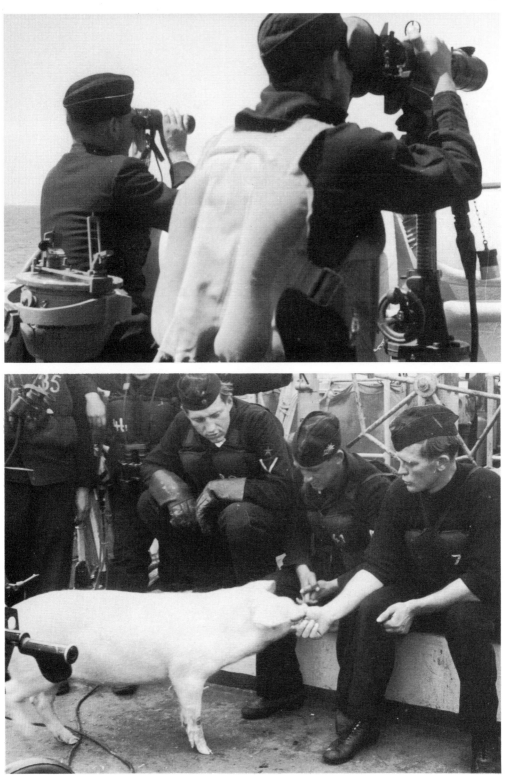

Above An action shot of the first order as a warrant officer fires a line to another warship at sea (112MW/5551/3).

Left The open steering position of an auxiliary minesweeper. Signal flags are stowed around the position and immediately behind the helmsman is a light anti-aircraft gun (129MW/6513/16).

Below Quite what these two are up to is unknown, but this shot does clearly show the trade/rank badge of a Chief Petty Officer yeoman (Schreiberobermaat)—an anchor with crossed quills, surmounting a chevron (MN/1579/21a).

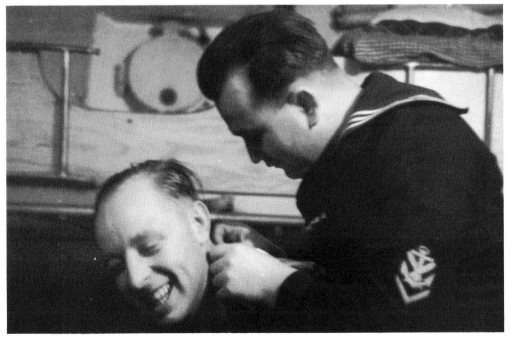

This page 'It's over here . . . no it's over there.' Lookouts on duty in a sweeper's crow's nest, keep watch for swept mines bobbing to the surface (129MW/6429/14/18 and 24).

Right A sweep in progress and the bridge crew keep watch for floating mines which have been swept by the preceding boats (115MW/5848/34a).

Below right A great variety of impressed local trading boats were drafted into the escort and minesweeping roles by the Kriegsmarine (113MW/5624/22a).

Left The crew of an auxiliary minesweeper (Sperrbrecher) enjoy a sing-song on the fo'c's'le (MW/6842/7a).

Below left The forward 3.7 cm dual-purpose mounting of a Sperrbrecher. Note the exposed position and the unarmoured bandstand (MW/6871/15).

Right A couple of the crewmembers of this auxiliary minesweeper wear blue pullover shirts—the most commonly worn item of naval clothing (MW/6797/23a).

Below These interesting uniforms are worn by members of the Zoll (Customs) service who are seen here examining the papers of a small fishing boat (100MW/4953/32).

Above An auxiliary minesweeper negotiates ice floes as it approaches the Baltic coast (112MW/5597/3a).

Below This auxiliary has run into ice and seems to be making heavy going of it (112MW/5597/7a).

This page Two former whale-catchers in service with the Kriegsmarine as escorts—note the flotilla commander's pennant (Flottillenstander) on the mainmast. These vessels fairly bristle with flak guns (111MW/5501/23a and MW/6358/6).

Above far left The bridge emblem on this auxiliary escort needs no explanation! The interesting thing is that this vessel is wearing the command flag of a Konter-Admiral at the masthead (129MW/6420/6a).

Above left The after end of a VP-boat where points of interest include the small outboard motor on the seaboat (left) and the covered muzzle of the 2 cm flak gun (155MW/5849/7).

Left Signs of severe icing can be seen on this VP-boat. These vessels gave sterling service as maids of all work during World War 2 (111MW/5529/27).

This page There were basically two types of Vorpostenboot used by the Kriegsmarine for escort duties—the impressed mercantile type (**above**) and the specially-built VP-boat, almost identical with their commercial counterparts. The pennant with an Iron Cross, worn on the mainmast of *VP401*, denotes the flotilla flagship (**right**) (113MW/5623/19 and 109MW/5416/2).

Inset A ceremonial occasion for auxiliary minesweepers. An inspection by a Kommodore (left) together with two Korvetten-Kapitäns and a minelaying specialist Leutnant zur See. The three more senior officers wear the badge for minesweepers, submarine hunters and security forces beneath their 1914 Iron Crosses. The two officers with white-covered caps also wear the 1939 clasp of the Iron Cross First Class (1914) above the actual Iron Cross (115MW/5849/25a).

Background photograph Watching the flotilla from the after gun bandstand during a North Sea sweep (129MW/6516/10a).

Above The building programme continued throughout the war period

Below Construction work on the coastal defences in progress; these works came under the jurisdiction of the local Coastal Commander (Küstenbefehlshaber) (M4KBK/17/829/10a).

Right Coastal defence batteries were to be found around Hitler's Fortress Europe and provided protection for friendly convoys and bases (M4KBK/17/829/22a).

Inset On shore support was provided by a multitude of bases and facilities, some even in the occupied countries. This photograph appears to show an engineering training school (112MW/5557/5).

1. Destroyers of the Kriegsmarine and their fates

Bombed: *Z1*; *Z3*; *Z23*; *Z24*; *Z28*.
Mined: *Z8*; *Z35*; *Z36*.
Gunfire: *Z7*; *Z16*; *Z26*; *Z27*; *Z32*.
Torpedoed: *Z19*; *Z21*; *Z22*.
Expended: *Z30* (as US Navy target).
Scuttled: *Z2*; *Z9*; *Z11*; *Z12*; *Z13*; *Z29*; *Z34*; *Z44*; *Z45*.
Scrapped: *Z4*; *Z5*; *Z6*; *Z10*; *Z14*; *Z15*; *Z17*; *Z18*; *Z20*; *Z25*; *Z31*; *Z33*; *Z37*; *Z38*; *Z43*; *Z46*; *Z47*; *Z51*.
Cancelled: *Z48*; *Z49*; *Z50*; *Z52*; *Z53*; *Z54*; *Z55*; *Z56*; *Z57*; *Z58*.

Notes
1. Losses at Narvik: *Z2*; *Z9*; *Z11*; *Z12*; *Z13*; *Z17*; *Z18*; *Z19*; *Z21*; *Z22*.
2. *Z39*'s last known fate was as a pier in France.
3. *Z40–Z42*, re-designated as cruisers but not completed.
4. *Z43* onwards did not see war service.

2. The fates of the Kriegsmarine's torpedo boats

Bombed: 11
Mined: 10
Gunfire: 4
Torpedoed: 4
Collision: 2
Scuttled: 7
Scrapped: 20

Notes
1. *T3* was sunk by bombing in 1941, later salvaged only to be mined in 1945.
2. 1941 type *T37–T51* destroyed and/or scuttled incomplete.
3. Older and former enemy torpedo boats have not been included.

3. The fates of the Kriegsmarine's major minesweepers

Bombed: 44
Mined: 11
Gunfire: 9
Sank: 2
Torpedoed: 13
Scrapped/
  Survived: 166
Scuttled: 16
Collision: 2
Cancelled: 593

ACHTUNG! COMPLETED YOUR COLLECTION?

Other titles in the same series

No 1 Panzers in the Desert
by Bruce Quarrie

No 2 German Bombers over England
by Bryan Philpott

No 3 Waffen-SS in Russia
by Bruce Quarrie

No 4 Fighters Defending the Reich
by Bryan Philpott

No 5 Panzers in North-West Europe
by Bruce Quarrie

No 6 German Fighters over the Med
by Bryan Philpott

No 7 German Paratroops in the Med
by Bruce Quarrie

No 8 German Bombers over Russia
by Bryan Philpott

No 9 Panzers in Russia 1941–43
by Bruce Quarrie

No 10 German Fighters over England
by Bryan Philpott

No 11 U-Boats in the Atlantic
by Paul Beaver

No 12 Panzers in Russia 1943–45
by Bruce Quarrie

No 13 German Bombers over the Med
by Bryan Philpott

No 14 German Capital Ships
by Paul Beaver

No 15 German Mountain Troops
by Bruce Quarrie

No 16 German Fighters over Russia
by Bryan Philpott

No 17 E-Boats and Coastal Craft
by Paul Beaver

No 18 German Maritime Aircraft
by Bryan Philpott

No 19 Panzers in the Balkans and Italy
by Bruce Quarrie

ACHTUNG! COMPLETED YOUR COLLECTION?